"Children and adults will love these gentle, empowering books. The Learning to Get Along series
powerful tool for teaching children essential social skills such as empathy, respect, cooperation, and
kindness. This straightforward and insightful series helps children visualize how their
appropriate behavior positively impacts themselves and others. I heartily recommend this
as a solid, classic resource for teaching affective skills to young children."

—Dr. Stephen R. Covey, Author, *The 7 Habits of Highly Effective People*

Learning
to Get
Along®

Share and Take Turns

Cheri J. Meiners, M.Ed.
Illustrated by Meredith Johnson

free spirit
PUBLISHING®

Library of Congress Cataloging-in-Publication Data
Meiners, Cheri J., 1957–
    Share and take turns / Cheri J. Meiners ; illustrations by Meredith Johnson.
        p. cm. —(Learning to get along)
Summary: Explains what sharing means and provides examples of different ways that two people can share what they both want, such as taking turns, dividing things, or playing together. Includes information and extension activities for parents or teachers.
    ISBN 1-57542-124-0
    1. Sharing—Juvenile literature. [1. Sharing. 2. Conduct of life.] I. Johnson, Meredith, ill. II. Title.
III. Series: Meiners, Cheri J., 1957–   Learning to get along.
BJ1533.G4 M45 2003
177'.7—dc21
                                                                                        2002153034
ISBN: 978-1-57542-124-7

Free Spirit Publishing does not have control over or assume responsibility for author or third-party websites and their content.

Reading Level Grade 1; Interest Level Ages 4–8; Fountas & Pinnell Guided Reading Level H

Cover and interior design by Marieka Heinlen
Edited by Marjorie Lisovskis

25 24 23 22
Printed in China
R18860421

Free Spirit Publishing Inc.
6325 Sandburg Road, Suite 100
Minneapolis, MN 55427-3674
(612) 338-2068
help4kids@freespirit.com
freespirit.com

Dedication

To Dad and Mom
for teaching me about sharing
and to
Vic, Rob, and Erik
for helping me
practice

Acknowledgments

I wish to thank Meredith Johnson for her beautiful illustrations. I also thank Judy Galbraith and all those at Free Spirit who believed in this series. Special thanks go to Marieka Heinlen for the lovely design and to Margie Lisovskis who, as editor, has contributed her wonderful expertise and creativity. Finally, I am grateful to Mary Jane Weiss, Ph.D., whose insight, skill, and caring have done much to advance the field of teaching social skills.

It's fun to play and imagine.

Sometimes when I play,
I want what other people have,

or they want what I have.

I know a way we can get along.
We can share.

One way to share is to divide things.

Another way to share is to use things together.

Playing together can be more fun than playing alone.

Trading is also a way to share.

My friend can use what I have,
while I use what my friend has.

Taking turns is a way of sharing, too.

When we can't use something at the same time, I can wait for my turn.

I can also share things I know.

And I can share special things about me, like things I make and do.

When I help someone, I share my time.

I might offer to share,
or another person might offer to share.

Sometimes I ask a friend to share.

I'm glad when someone shares with me.

If the person says no,
I can do something else.

It's not always easy to share.

I might have something that's special to me.

I might not want to share it.

Or I may not feel ready to share.

That's okay.

I can choose
not to
share . . .

or offer to share later . . .

or share something else.

Sometimes, I decide to share
even though it's hard for me.

When I share or take turns,
I'm being generous.

I'm learning to make good choices.

I'm learning to think about others.

No matter where I am, or who I'm with,

there are special ways that I can share.

Ways to Reinforce the Ideas in *Share and Take Turns*

As you read each page spread, ask children:

• What's happening in this picture?

Here are additional questions you might discuss:

Page 1

• Why are these children having a good time?

Pages 2–3

• Who could share in this picture? What could that person do?

• Have you ever wanted to play with something another person was using? What happened?

Pages 4–11

• What is sharing?

• How are these children sharing?

• What are some other things we (you) can share by dividing? use together? share by trading?

• How does taking turns help people get along? *(Include in your discussion the idea of being fair. Also discuss some situations where there may be several possible ways to share.)*

Pages 12–15

• When have you shared something you know? Something you made?

• When have you shared by helping someone or doing something for another person?

• What are some ways you share at school (at home, outside, in other settings)?

Pages 16–21

• What are some times you can offer to share with someone else? How can you offer? What can you say?

• What are some times you might ask someone to share with you? How can you ask? What can you say?

• What can you say if the person says yes?

• What can you say if the person says no? What can you do instead? *(In discussing ways to ask and offer, talk about the importance of being friendly and polite. For example, instead of, "Gimme that book—I want it!" people are more likely to want to share when asked, "Could I please see that?" or, "Will you be done soon? Can I use it then?" Help children understand that being courteous when talking about sharing is a way to show respect.)*

Pages 22–27

• When is it hard to share? Why is it hard?

• If you don't want to share something, what can you say? What can you do?

- What are some things that you *shouldn't* share? *(Often medical or health reasons such as allergies dictate rules about what should not be shared. For example, at school, children may be told not to share combs, hats, or food. At home, children may be told not to drink from someone else's cup. Be clear in this discussion about things that children should not share and what they can say when someone asks them to share any of these things.)*
- Have you ever shared something when it was hard to do? What happened? How did you feel? How did the other person feel?
- Has anyone ever shared something with you even though it was hard to share? What happened? How did you feel?
- What does it mean to be generous? *(Children might suggest being kind, sharing, and being willing to let others play with them or use their things. You might also discuss the opposite of being generous: being selfish. At the same time, make it clear that while it's good to be generous, no one is expected to be generous with everything all the time.)*

Pages 28–29

- How do you decide to share or not share?
- Why is it important to think about others?

Pages 30–31

- Where are some places you can share?
- Who are people you can share with? What can you share?
- What are some special ways you can share? *(Help children think about personalized ways they can share. Children can share things they make, such as pictures, puppets, clay figures, or food. They can share ideas about ways to use a toy or solve a problem. They can also share skills or talents—for example, by showing a younger sibling how to print letters, or by singing or teaching others a song. The idea is to help children identify a range of ways to share and also ways of sharing that are uniquely theirs.)*

Sharing Games

Read this book often with your child or group of children. Once children are familiar with the book, refer to it when teachable moments arise involving positive behavior or problems related to sharing and taking turns. Make it a point to notice and comment when children share and take turns. In addition, use the following activities to reinforce children's understanding of how to share and take turns.

Ways to Share Game

Materials: Pictures of toys and small items cut from magazines and catalogs; bag to hold the pictures; whiteboard with magnets, or 4 index cards

Level 1

Review pages 4–11 with your child or group of children, making sure they understand the different ways to share that are described. Then have a child draw a toy from the bag. Ask: "How can you share this?" or "How can (child's name) share this?" Be open to more than one possible way to share the item. Follow-up questions you might ask include: "Who could you share this with?" or "Is this something you would share?" Repeat with other toys from the bag.

Level 2

Write the words *Divide, Use Together, Trade,* and *Take Turns* on the board, or write one term on each index card and lay the cards on the table. Follow the procedures for Level 1, this time having the child explain how to share the item and place its picture under the appropriate term on the board or on the appropriate index card.

Sharing Role Plays

Materials (Levels 1 and 2): One copy of the stick-puppet template (from digital content; see page 35) for each child and yourself; crayons or markers; other materials for decorating (yarn, glitter, construction paper); scissors; Popsicle sticks; glue; pictures of toys and small items cut from magazines and catalogs; small self-stick notes or two-sided removable tape (for attaching the pictures to the puppets so the stick characters can "hold" the toys)

Preparation (Levels 1 and 2): Cut out more pictures than there are people in your group (you may also draw pictures of toys and other items if you prefer); glue the pictures to self-stick notes or put the two-sided removable tape on the back of each picture. With children, color, cut out, and decorate the stick puppets. Glue the puppets to the sticks.

Level 1

Review a scene from the book and have children in groups of two or three enact it, using the toys described or other favorite items. (Not all materials will be appropriate for all ways of sharing.) Repeat this with several scenes from the book.

Level 2

Form groups of two or three children and give each group one picture. Then call out a direction, such as "Offer to trade" or "Ask if you can have a turn." Have children take turns using their stick puppets to role play as directed, switching roles so all children get a chance to have their puppets play different parts. Continue to role play and have children role play scenes in which the puppets:

• offer to share or invite someone to take part

• ask if they may share or have a turn

• find ways to share and take turns

• find ways to solve problems when someone doesn't want to share or take turns

Level 3

With children in groups of two or three, describe a scenario using dolls or stuffed animals. You might say, "Tootie is playing with the truck. Big Bear wants to use the truck, too. How can they use it together?" Invite children's ideas, and ask about other ways the truck can be shared.

Then have children role play this and other scenes using dolls, action figures, and stuffed animals who are playing with toys from your classroom or home. Start with neutral toys that are not favorites; then move to toys that are often in demand or that children find difficult to share. Encourage children to practice ways to ask or offer to share; ways to share by dividing, using together, trading, and taking turns; and ways to solve problems when someone doesn't want to share or isn't ready to do so.

When a problem arises that involves sharing or taking turns, use the stick puppets, dolls, or stuffed animals to role play ways to deal with the situation, or have children enact solutions.

Sharing Poster

Materials: Posterboard, crayons or markers, glue sticks, scissors, pictures cut from magazines or catalogs showing people sharing or items that can be shared, word strips (see "Preparation")

Preparation: Print words on strips of paper. Level 1 words: *take turns, divide, trade, use together.* Level 2 words: *cooperation, respect, generosity, fairness.*

Directions: Ask children to share materials and draw or paste pictures of people sharing to create a large poster together. Allow children to be imaginative and to add any pictures to the poster that depict things they would like to share if they could.

Level 1
Discuss the Level 1 words in relation to the poster. Add them to parts of the poster that demonstrate those aspects of sharing.

Level 2
Discuss the Level 2 words. Talk about the principles involved in the scenarios on the poster, or have children label them. ("Tips for Sharing" in the digital content includes additional ideas about teaching cooperation, respect, generosity, and fairness. See below for information on accessing the digital content.)

Handmade Sharing Bags

Materials: *For each bag:* piece of fabric measuring at least 18" on each side (such as a 20" x 20" bandana; a "fat quarter" of cotton fabric, which is precut to 18" x 22"; or a clean dish towel), large needle, matching thread, scissors. *For the bag closure:* a strip of stick-on hook-and-loop fasteners or chenille stem wire to twist on at the top. *For the handle (optional):* ribbon.

Preparation: Ask children to bring a small personal nonfood item that they are willing to share. It should fit into the bag they will make. Be sure you have enough adult helpers to assist children with the sewing part of the activity.

Directions: To make the bag, place children in small groups. Help each child make a bag. Select a piece of cloth and fold it in half with the wrong sides together. Thread a needle and tie both ends of the thread together so that the thread is doubled. Have or help the child sew two adjacent sides of the fabric together, leaving one side open. Turn bags right side out. For the closure, choose an option listed in "Materials." You may also wish to add a handle or another embellishment. Have children place their sharing items in their bags and close the bags. Explain that the bag can be reused with new items when you want to repeat the activity.

Level 1
With children in pairs, ask them to talk together and share their items, allowing their partner to hold the item. Ask, "How did it feel to share and talk about your item? How do you feel when someone shares with you?"

Level 2
With children in small groups, form circles and ask children, one at a time, to pass their bag with the object around the circle for others in their group to open and hold. Encourage children to respond positively to the owner about the object. You might ask children, "How can sharing your item show cooperation? Respect? Generosity?"

For additional information, download the stick-puppet template, "Tips for Sharing," and "More Sharing Games" at freespirit.com/share; **use the password** 2gether.

Free Spirit's Learning to Get Along® Series

Help children learn, understand, and practice basic social and emotional skills. Real-life situations, diversity, and concrete examples make these read-aloud books appropriate for childcare settings, schools, and the home. *Each book: 40 pp., color illust., PB, 9" x 9", ages 4–8.*

Each book: 48 pp., color illust., PB, 9" x 9", ages 4–8.

See more Learning to Get Along® bilingual editions at freespirit.com